Raleigh, Durham, Chapel Hill

A PHOTOGRAPHIC PORTRAIT

PHOTOGRAPHY BY EDWIN MORGAN

First published in the United States of
America by:

Twin Lights Publishers, Inc.
8 Hale Street
Rockport, Massachusetts 01966
Telephone: (978) 546-7398
http://www.twinlightspub.com

ISBN: 1-885435-67-3
ISBN: 978-1-885435-67-5

10 9 8 7 6 5 4 3 2 1

Opposite:

PIEDMONT NATURE TRAIL

In the middle of the gardens, visitors can
hike a two-mile trail through eighty-eight
acres of forest that is typical of central
North Carolina. Benches provide a place to
stop and enjoy nature's abundant beauty.

Editorial researched and
written by:
Francesca and Duncan Yates
www.freelancewriters.com

Book design by:
SYP Design & Production, Inc.
www.sypdesign.com

Printed in China

Raleigh, Durham, Chapel Hill

East of the Great Smokey Mountains, on the rolling, green hills of North Carolina's Piedmont, lies one of America's most unique phenomena, known simply as "The Triangle."

Anchored at three corners by Raleigh, Durham, and the college town of Chapel Hill, The Triangle is home to an unprecedented concentration of some of the most brilliant researchers, scientists, medical practitioners, and educators in the country. This massive think tank, a deliberate collaboration of universities and industries, is responsible for many high-tech products and innovations that continue to change lives throughout the global community.

Filled with the evocative work of Raleigh native, Edwin Morgan, these photographs provide an intimate tour of the exceptional communities of the Triangle.

Raleigh

Raleigh was specifically built in 1792 as the state capitol. Today, it is home to over 300,000 people and is best known as the creator of Research Triangle Park, the largest research park in the world.

Morgan's camera takes you inside the State Capitol, research-powerhouse North Carolina State University, and Raleigh's world-class museums, with their highly-acclaimed collections of art, natural history, and science. Learn about Raleigh's favorite festivals, and endulge in her pristine parks and outdoor spaces.

Durham

Walk the historic grounds of the birthplace of America's tobacco industry—the modest farm of Washington Duke—where the first crops of marketable tobacco grew out of a rich soil, perfect for the task.

Durham was the lucky recipient of the Duke family's boundless philanthropy, most notably Duke University, with its world-ranked medical center. Now known as the "City of Medicine," Durham hosts over three-hundred health and medicine related companies.

Chapel Hill

Chapel Hill is home to the first public university in the country, UNC-Chapel Hill. It was the only one to award degrees to students in the 18th century.

Morgan's lens explores the forested grounds of one of the most beautiful campuses in the nation, where 27,000 students and a faculty of three thousand create a learning environment of world-class excellence.

This richly-photographed tour of "The Triangle," beautifully depicts one of America's most fascinating metropolises.

North Carolina State Bell Tower

Plans were launched in 1919 for a bell tower that would serve as a memorial for alumni who had died in WWI. After numerous delays and another world war, the bell tower was finally completed thirty years later.

Historic Tucker House *(above and opposite)*

At the turn of the 20th century, Blount Street was the most fashionable neighborhood in Raleigh, and the Tucker House was one of its grand homes. It is a striking example of Neo-Classical Revival architecture.

The elegant residence is richly detailed with hardwood floors, mahogany woodwork and dark paneling. Interesting features include a library, radio room, telephone room, and butler's pantry.

THE
TUCKER
HOUSE

Oakwood·Mordecai
Meeting House

418 N. Person St.

Raleigh Parks and
Recreation Department

Executive Mansion, Raleigh

The governor's mansion (1891), in the fashionable Blount Street historic district, is one of the state's most striking examples of Victorian Queen Anne architecture. Michael Easley is the twenty-seventh governor to live there.

Mordecai Historic Park

Originally one of the largest planta-
tions in Wake County, the 1785
Mordecai House is one of Raleigh's
oldest residences. President Andrew
Johnson's birthplace was moved to
these grounds in the early 20th century.

Fannie Heck Historical Marker *(above)*

The highway marker honors Fannie Heck, who lived in this house when she founded the North Carolina Woman's Missionary Union, a Baptist organization. She served as president from 1886 until her death in 1915.

Heck-Andrews House *(opposite)*

Shortly after the end of the Civil War, a successful armaments manufacturer named Jonathan Heck built one of the first, post-war, grand residences in Raleigh and set the tone for the well-to-do neighborhood.

State Legislative Building

Designed by Edward Durell Stone in 1963 in a blend of modern and classical architectural styles, the Raleigh building is unique because it is solely used by the legislative branch of government.

Vietnam Veteran's Memorial

"After the Firefight" depicts the first Native-American and African-American to be honored by a monument on Raleigh's Union Square. The monument was designed by North Carolina sculptor Abbe Godwin.

Women of the Confederacy (top)

This poignant statue on State House grounds depicts the futility of war. A mother reads her son a story about the sacrifices of war. He listens, grasping a sword that he will use when he goes off to battle as a young man.

George Washington (bottom)

The statue depicts Washington as a Roman officer, writing the first words of his farewell address. It is a copy of the original statue by master sculptor Antonio Canova which resided in the original state house from 1820–1831.

Ensign Worth Bagley

Son of a prominent Raleigh family, Ensign Bagley was the first Naval officer killed in the Spanish-American War. It is one of several statues on the state house grounds that honor fallen sons and daughters of the South.

15

State Capitol

This Greek Revival structure was built in a cross style, with a domed rotunda in the center, connecting the four wings. The old legislative chambers and other rooms have been restored to their original 1840's appearance.

One of America's Best Cities

Raleigh's population has risen to
approximately 350,000, making it one
of the fastest growing cities in the
country. Combined with its sister
cities, Durham and Cary, the population is over one-and-one-half million.

Martin Luther King Memorial Gardens *(top)*

This life-sized likeness of Dr. Martin Luther King, Jr. is mounted on the ground making it more accessible to the public. Children, especially, enjoy holding Dr. King's outstretched hand.

"Let Freedom Ring" *(bottom)*

This evocative park opened in Raleigh in 1989 as the first public park in the country dedicated exclusively to civil rights leader, Dr. Martin Luther King, Jr. and the civil rights movement.

...UNTIL
JUSTICE ROLLS
DOWN LIKE WATERS
AND RIGHTEOUSNESS
LIKE A MIGHTY STREAM.
DR. MARTIN LUTHER KING, JR.

Memorial Fountain

Water flows softly over the surface of a twelve-ton, granite monument, inscribed with the names of civil rights pioneers. The King Memorial Wall surrounds his statue with 2,400 bricks naming the park's supporters.

Moore Square *(top and bottom)*

One of Raleigh's four original public squares designed in 1792, Moore Square is the center of a vibrant, revitalized area that includes City Market, Exploris Museum, shops, art galleries and restaurants. The Square hosts anticipated festivals such as the Artsplosure, an outdoor arts festival that features hundreds of visual and performing artists and First Night, Raleigh's world-famous New Year's Eve celebration.

"Acorn," Moore Square

This ten-foot-tall sculpture was designed to commemorate Raleigh's bicentennial in 1992. A fitting tribute to the "City of Oaks," the copper acorn glows at night when floodlights transform it into a shimmering beacon.

North Carolina State Fair, Raleigh

Wild rides aren't the only attraction at the state fair. Numerous food booths offer every mouth-watering snack your taste buds can imagine. Kids know that on "fair day," their parents will give in to their sweet-tooth demands.

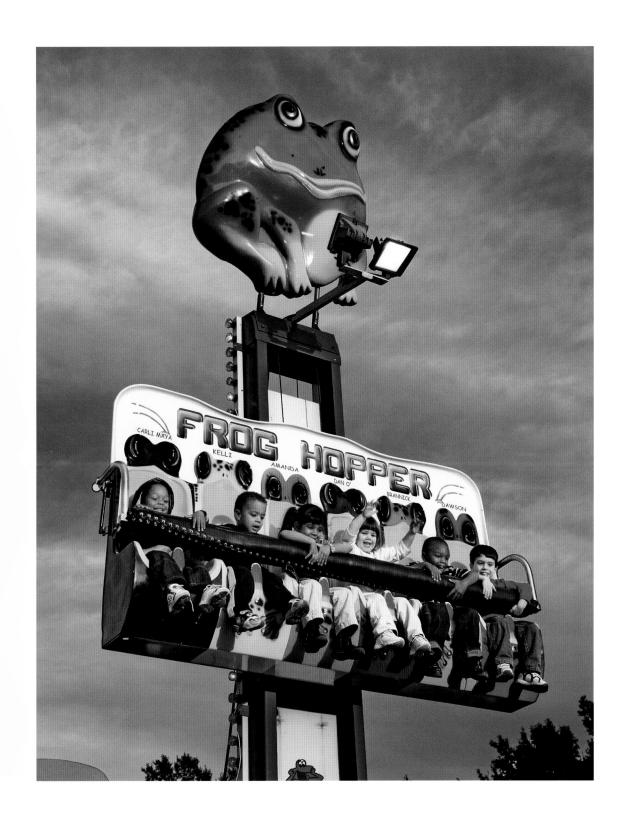

Pint-Sized Thrills

Back in 1891, curious fairgoers climbed aboard "Switchback Railroad," the first midway ride built on the fairgrounds. Today there are thrill rides for all ages, depending on your courage and, of course, your height.

State Farmer's Market (top and bottom)

A friendly vendor tempts passersby with fresh, vine-ripened tomatoes at Raleigh's sprawling farmers market. Sponsored by the North Carolina Department of Agriculture, this 75-acre market showcases a delectable spread of local produce in comfortable, climate-controlled spaces. Gardeners can find the season's best plants, trees and flowers. Special events highlight fruits and vegetables at their peak times.

Orange Harvest (opposite)

October is a fun-filled month at the market. Kids' activities include contests and prize money for the largest and best-decorated pumpkin, a Halloween Haunted House, a moon-walk, and musical entertainment.

Future Favorites in Bloom *(top)*

Filled with blooming plants all year round, the Plant Trials area at Raleigh's J.C. Raulston Arboretum tests new cultivars of bedding plants. It is one of the national testing sites designated by All-America Selections.

Cool Oasis *(bottom)*

Children dip their hands into a cool pond at the Arboretum, one of many water features on display that inspire homeowners with landscaping ideas. Free tours are offered every Sunday afternoon from March to October.

J.C. Raulston Arboretum *(opposite)*

The arboretum garden is a nationally-acclaimed research and teaching garden of North Carolina State University's horticulture department. It showcases the most varied selection of superior plants for southeastern landscaping.

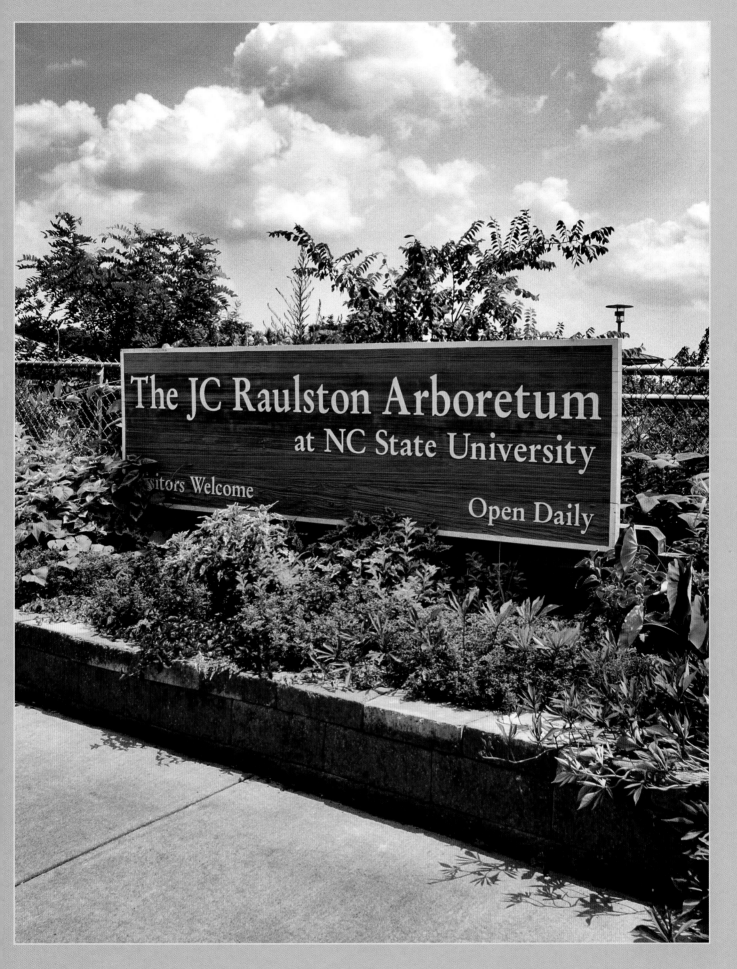

The JC Raulston Arboretum
at NC State University

Visitors Welcome

Open Daily

An Afternoon Stroll

One of Raleigh's scenic city parks,
Shelly Lake, features deep, green
woods and a beautiful lake for swimming, boating and fishing. Visitors can
enjoy a slow walk or a fast jog on the
two-mile lakeside trail.

Art in the Park *(top)*

The Sertoma Arts Center, located in this Raleigh park, is the perfect place to indulge in artistic pleasures and find new outlets for your creativity. Classes in photography, painting, drawing, and pottery are available.

William B. Umstead State Park *(bottom)*

The serene, natural beauty of these deep woods where visitors can hike, fish, or ride horseback along trails, is surprisingly surrounded by the metropolises of Raleigh, Durham, Cary and Research Triangle Park.

Pullen Park, Raleigh

Even today, seventy-five cents still buys a magical ride on the back of a tiger, horse or other animal kingdom favorites. This Raleigh park's vintage 1912 carousel is on the National Register of Historic Sites.

A Walk in the Park

In the heart of Raleigh is a sprawling oasis of nature that attracts over a million visitors yearly. Paddle boats, greenways, a swimming pool, playgrounds, tennis courts and an amusement park make it a top attraction.

North Carolina Museum of History

This prolific museum is filled with artifacts and exhibits from yesteryear and
present-day North Carolina, as diverse
as World War II spy gadgets and
Richard Petty's stock car.

Six Centuries of History

Since 1902, this state museum has amassed a diverse collection of more than 150,000 artifacts of North Carolina life over six centuries. The museum provides backpacks filled with activities for their young visitors.

Flying High Through History *(above)*

Suspended above the museum lobby is this authentic Gyro-Copter, a flying machine invented by Raleigh's Igor Benson. Nearby is a replica of the Wright Brothers' 1903 plane that conquered gravity above the Outer Banks.

North Carolina Treasures *(opposite)*

Journalist and history buff, Fred Olds wrote newspaper articles about the state's history in the late 20th century. He asked readers to bring their artifacts to him. Soon he had collected enough to open the Hall of History in 1902. He ran the museum for 32 years and personally collected nearly 30,000 artifacts. Some were strange, but many were genuine treasures. Most important, Olds excited the public about the history of their great state.

North Carolina State University

Founded in 1887, North Carolina State is a nationally recognized research university and the largest in the state, with over 30,000 students enrolled. It is known for its design, agriculture, engineering, and textile programs.

Centennial Campus

Centennial Campus is the university's
world-class research park where over a
hundred businesses and government
agencies partner with university faculty
to produce scientific and technical
innovations. Hundreds of patents and
dozens of new companies have
evolved out of this high-tech incuba-
tor over the past two decades, collec-
tively providing thousands of jobs in
pharmaceuticals, textiles, software,
and environmental engineering.

Terror of the South

Nicknamed Acro, or "Terror of the South," this giant, prehistoric animal is a top attraction at the North Carolina Museum of Natural Sciences. This is the only skeleton on display anywhere in the world of Acrocanthosaurus Atokensis, a 110-million-year-old predatory dinosaur. At 13 feet tall and forty feet long, Acro towers over neighboring exhibits of 200 species of live animals including hellbender salamanders and two-toed sloths.

Museum of Natural Sciences

The largest natural history museum in the Southeast is also the most-visited museum in North Carolina. After 121 years, the Raleigh museum moved to this splendid, new building, quadrupling the size of its previous quarters.

With four floors of exhibits, live animals, and exciting hands-on activities, the museum provides a unique view of the natural world by studying North Carolina's diverse geography, geology, plants and animals.

ONE
VOICE
FROM THE PEN OF

Anne Frank

STAMP
Art

BERLIN WALL
WEST BERLIN
SIDE   1961 - 1989

DIE BERLINER
MAUER
WESTBERLINER
SEITE

Exploris Museum *(opposite)*

Visitors to this provocative, interactive museum step into the virtual worlds of neighbors around the globe via hands-on lessons about Earth's natural resources, dancing in other countries and touching the Berlin Wall.

North Carolina Museum of Art *(above)*

This internationally acclaimed museum contains a collection of art and artifacts that spans five-thousand years. It is best known in art circles for its remarkable collection of European paintings and sculpture.

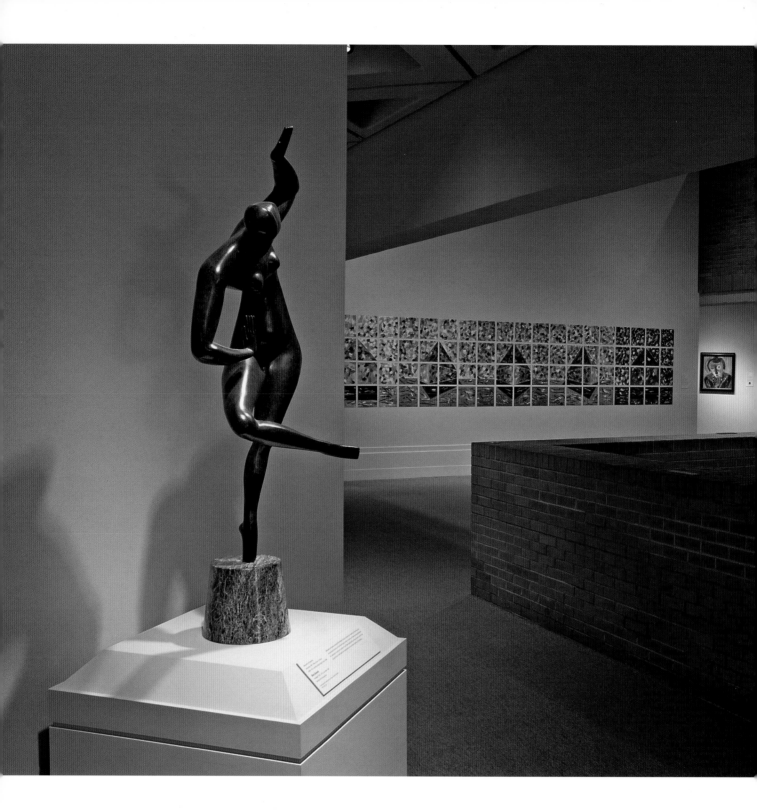

"Blue Dancer"

The North Carolina Museum of Art's contemporary collection highlights major works by European and American artists such as Ernst Ludwig Kirchner and Marsden Hartley. Above is "Blue Dancer," by Alexander Archipenko.

Art Across the Ages

The museum display works from Ancient Egypt through centuries of European art, with important pieces by Giotto, Botticelli, Raphael, Peter Paul Rubens, Anthony van Dyck, Antionio Canova and Claude Monet.

Bennett Place *(above, left and opposite)*

Seventeen days after General Robert E. Lee surrendered at Appomattox, Confederate General Joseph E. Johnston negotiated the largest and final troop surrender of the Civil War at Durham's Bennett Place.

Living History *(above and opposite)*

Every Wednesday visitors to the farm-
stead at Bennett Place can observe
early American life, including daily
chores, gardening, cooking, spinning,
washing, and children playing games
that were popular in the 19th-century.

Duke Homestead and Tobacco Museum *(above)*

This remarkable museum exhibits 19th-century artifacts and archives, while the Duke Homestead tells the personal story of Durham icon and tobacco farmer, Washington Duke.

Birth of the Tobacco Industry *(opposite)*

Visitors to the Homestead take a fascinating walk back in time to the birthplace of the modern tobacco industry in the early 1800's. The original Duke residence and several out-buildings are on display.

Tobacco Harvesting *(top)*

The historic homestead hosts many popular annual events such as a Tobacco Harvest Festival and Mock Tobacco Auction in September and an Herb, Garden, and Craft Festival in June.

Tobacco Farm Chores *(bottom)*

Those attending the Homestead's special events and festivals can observe a 19th-century tobacco farm in action, from harvesting to curing the world-famous North Carolina bright leaf tobacco.

Duke Homestead

After the Civil War, the Duke family returned to find their small farm ravaged. Fortunately, the Yankees had overlooked a small quantity of leaf tobacco, enough to eventually begin manufacturing "Pro Bono Publico," a smoking tobacco. Success was immediate everywhere it was introduced. Eventually, the Duke family formed the American Tobacco Company and went on to control ninety percent of worldwide tobacco sales.

Prominent Tobacco

James A. Bonsack

James B. Duke

R. J. Rey

Bonsack patented a cigarette machine in 1880 that initially performed the work of 48 hand-rollers. A second, improved machine was patented in 1881. The Bonsack machine revolutionized the production of cigarettes and paved the way for mechanization of the entire tobacco industry.

Buck Duke began his career in his father's company, W. Duke & Sons, and became a partner at the age of 18. In 1890 he formed the giant American Tobacco Company by a merger of the five largest cigarette manufacturers. Because of Duke's marketing and organizational skills, the American Tobacco Company rose to dominate the world's tobacco industry for two decades.

Duke Homestead Tobacco Museum

This modern museum tells the fascinating story of the Duke family and the birth and growth of the tobacco industry, using a combination of historic artifacts and photographs, multimedia and animatronics displays.

Modified Hungarian-shaped Pipe
Briar bowl with BBB trademark
("Britain's Best Briars," England's
oldest trademark, dates from
1847). Probably made by
Cadogan, England; circa 1950.

Pipe
Made by Vienna Company, U.S.;
circa 1950. The white meerschaum
bowl has yellowed from use.

Sepiolite (meerschaum)

nalities

John Walton

George M. H

Early Advertising

Historic Tobacco Pipes *(top)*

The craftsmanship of fine tobacco
pipes are among many exhibits that
showcase a wide variety of smoking
paraphernalia, including meerschaum
pipes and the elegant, 19th-century
"Britain's Best Briars" pipes.

Tobacco Advertisments *(bottom)*

Advertisements for The Pride of
Durham and other historic tobacco
brands are displayed throughout the
museum. The image of tobacco was
initially crafted to appeal to men, and
later, to women as well.

Great Barn, Durham

The surviving structures of Historic Stagville provide a fascinating view of a pre-Civil War southern plantation. Built in 1860 by slave craftsmen, the Great Barn was the largest building in North Carolina devoted to agriculture.

Historic Stagville

When the Civil War began, Stagville had nearly nine-hundred slaves tending crops in fields that covered 30,000 acres. Established in the late 1700's, Stagville become the largest plantation in North Carolina.

Museum of Life and Science, Durham

The Magic Wings Butterfly House is just one of the many interesting exhibits in this interactive museum. Here, the joy of experiencing the natural world is celebrated with up-close experiences in state-of-the-art exhibits.

Colors in Nature

In a lush setting of exotic plants at the Museum of Life and Science are a thousand butterflies from all over the world. Exquisitely patterned insects emerge from their chrysalises to display their pageantry.

Durham Central Park *(above)*

A key part of Durham's master plan for revitalizing downtown neighborhoods, Durham Central Park is a new, five-acre park that provides a community venue for cultural and outdoor activities for the area.

West Point on the Eno *(opposite)*

Located on a protected stretch of the Eno River, this historic park has hiking trails, a working blacksmith shop and a reconstructed grist mill that grinds corn and wheat. Sherman's cavalry camped here at the end of war.

Sarah P. Duke Gardens

Adjacent to renowned Duke University
Medical Center is one of the finest
public gardens in the country. Known
for the brilliance of its landscape
design and horticultural expertise, the
gardens are a top Durham attraction.

A Fulfilling Garden Experience

Walk along the gardens' meandering pathways through woodlands and formal plantings. Rest at a gazebo draped with sweet, fragrant wisteria, and lunch at the Terrace Café amidst nature at its best.

Duke University Chapel *(above)*

Gracing the highest ridge on campus with spires rising over one hundred feet, this neo-Gothic chapel is the legacy of the University's founder, James B. Duke, who died ten years before the chapel was completed.

Soaring to the Heavens *(opposite)*

This magnificent structure of volcanic North Carolina stone was the first built on the new University campus in 1930. Its monumental tower would normally grace a large Gothic cathedral, not a smaller chapel such as this.

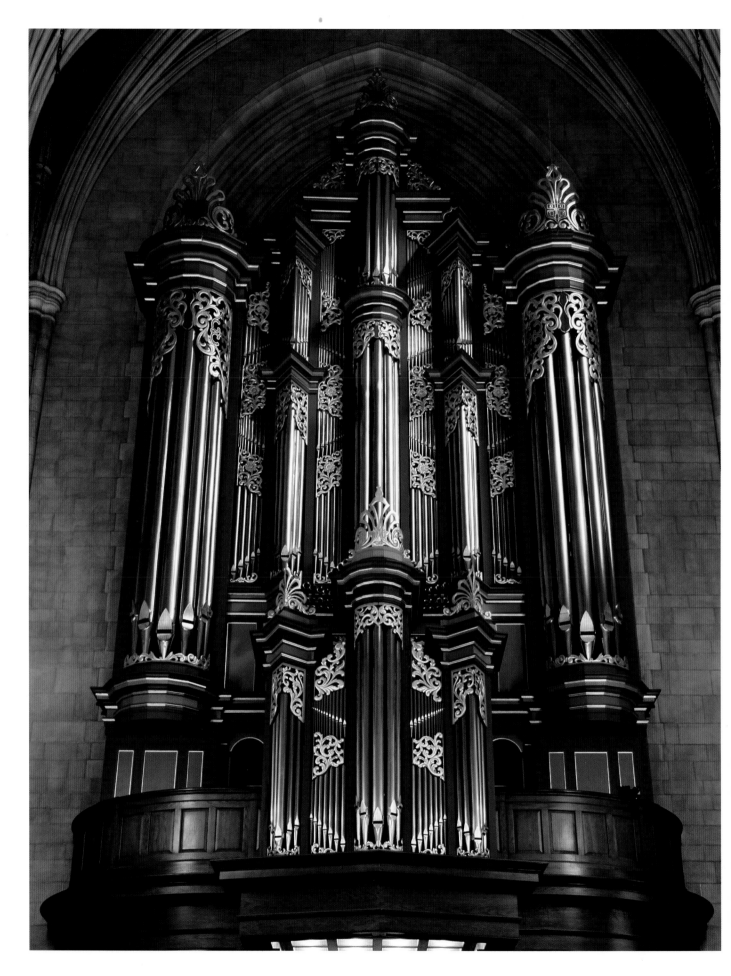

Musical Magnificence *(opposite)*

When the air fills with the magnificent sounds of Duke Chapel's famous Flentrop Organ, it is the same tonal experience as hearing Bach's music played in 18th-century Europe during the golden age of the organ.

Bible Stories in Glass *(above)*

Seventy-seven stained glass windows grace this magnificent chapel and depict every major scene in the Bible. In the style of French Gothic cathedrals, the scenes feature stylized figures and bright colors.

Brightleaf Square

At the turn of the 20th century, this trendy shopping area in Durham's revitalized downtown area was the state's first commercial district with warehouses bustling with tobacco industry activity.

A New Downtown Look

The former warehouses of the American Tobacco Company are now home to an upscale shopping complex. Brightleaf Square shops are filled with antiques, clothing, rare books, and much more.

Carolina Theatre

The Carolina Theatre incorporates a neo-classical and beaux-arts style that was popular in 1925. Along with the stylized interior is an Egyptian influence resulting from the discovery of King Tut's tomb in 1922. Crossed, golden shafts of wheat and a subtle dogwood pattern are entwined by blue ribbons on either side of the stage. The multi-million-dollar renovation, completed in 1994, enhances the theatre's heritage.

Heritage on Stage

The city of Durham's renovation of this vintage theatre is one important part of the master plan to strategically revitalize the downtown area and, at the same time, restore the symbols of its rich heritage.

City of Medicine *(above)*

Durham is synonymous with state-of-the-art medical services, with more than three hundred health-related companies and medical practices employing one third of the population.

Duke Children's Hospital *(opposite)*

Durham has many top-ranked medical and research facilities, as well as diet and fitness centers. Duke Children's Hospital is one of the nation's best with innovative services, cutting-edge technology and a top-notch staff.

Bimbé Festival *(top)*

Sponsored by the Hayti Cultural Center, Bimbé is one of the oldest cultural festivals in the country and one of the region's biggest. This free annual event attracts loyal fans to Durham every year.

Arts and Crafts *(bottom)*

Festival exhibits celebrate the rich arts and crafts traditions of African and Caribbean culture. Lively colors and fine details of the hand-painted plates and other wares convey a distinct ethinc heritage.

Modern and Traditional *(top)*

Bimbé is a joyous celebration of the energizing music, art, dance and clothing styles found throughout African and Caribbean cultures. Traditions from distant lands are passed down to future generations.

The Rhythm of Bimbé Festival *(bottom)*

Music is everywhere at the Bimbé Festival where visitors dance or just tap their feet to the hypnotic rhythms of hip-hop, jazz, blues, gospel music and hot Latin beats with a distinctive Caribbean flavor.

Streets of Southpoint, Durham

USA Today featured this new downtown attraction as one of "Ten Great Places to Spend It All in One Place." Making headlines are over 140 unique shops and restaurants, along with major department stores.

Forever Young

Children at play are immortalized in this fantastic water-fountain sculpture. The colorful casts convey the light-hearted innocence of chilidhood and bring out the child in all who enjoy them.

Durham Armory

The old Durham Armory is one of five
buildings in the city's downtown Civic
Center Complex. Strategically located
in the center of the arts and historic
districts, the Armory has a large audi-
torium/ballroom and meeting rooms.

North Carolina Central University

In 1910, this Durham university was
founded as a state liberal arts college
for African Americans. It is now a
regional university, open to all ethnici-
ties, with graduate programs in law,
business, education, arts and science.

Durham Bulls Athletic Park

The Bulls have been a minor league
baseball tradition since 1902 and
began playing in their new athletic
park in 1995. Hundreds of Bulls
players have gone on to distinguish
themselves in the majors.

Wool E. Bull

The Duham Bulls' mascot is a celebrity amongst baseball mascots. Wool E. Bull has been voted onto the ballot for the Mascot Hall of Fame. Out of six professionals, he's the only Minor League mascot on the ballot.

Hayti Heritage Center (above)

This vivacious cultural center, carved out of an historic sanctuary, pays tribute to the dignity and resolve of a Durham neighborhood once recognized as the most prosperous African-American community in the nation.

Windows of Heritage (opposite)

The Hayti Heritage Center is housed in historic St. Joseph's AME Church, an outstanding Gothic structure built in 1891. Elaborate stained glass windows memorialize major church contributors and tell Biblical stories.

Ackland Museum *(above)*

Located on the UNC campus, the Ackland Museum's permanent collection includes over 15,000 art objects from Asia, Africa, and America. It is renowned for its prominent European painting and sculpture collections.

"Head of Buddha" *(opposite)*

The Ackland Museum has the most significant collection of Asian art in the state. "Head of the Buddha" a 15th-century bronze carving from Thailand (*foreground*), is the only one of its kind in the United States.

Final Resting Place

Even though William Ackland was not an art collector, he wanted the people of his native South to know and love fine arts. He bequeathed his fortune to establishing the Ackland Museum and stipulated that he be buried inside.

Art Appreciation

As part of UNC-Chapel Hill, Ackland Museum's mission is to create a provocative environment for the learning and appreciation of art for students, faculty and the public.

Kenan Football Center

Named after a generous benefactor, the $50-million-dollar Frank H. Kenan Football Center and Sports Museum at U.N.C.-Chapel Hill houses what is widely considered to be the best football facility in the nation.

THE WORLD'S LARGEST RAM
PRESENTED TO THE UNIVERSITY AND
ITS ATHLETIC TEAMS WITH PRIDE BY
IRWIN BELK - CLASS OF 1945,
WILLIAM IRWIN BELK - CLASS OF 1971,
MARILYN BELK WALLIS - CLASS OF 1975,
CARL G. BELK - CLASS OF 1982, AND
ANNE REYNOLDS BELK - CLASS OF 1985

Dedicated: November 19, 2002
Sculptor: Kent Ullberg

"Ramses," the Mascot

From the start, Ramses has been good
luck for the Tarheels. When the ram
walked onto the field as the official
mascot in 1924, the team's unrelenting
slump was magically broken with a
perfect drop kick in the fourth quarter.

Kenan Sports Museum

The Kenan Football Center's Sports
Museum showcases sports memora-
bilia and a multi-media history of the
Carolina Tarheels. Eighteen outstand-
ing players have earned a place in its
Hall of Fame.

An Historic Dormitory

When UNC opened in 1793, it was the young nation's first public institution of higher education. "Old East" was its first and only structure and was built near an Anglican chapel in what became the town of Chapel Hill.

Ayr Mount, Hillsborough *(above)*

Ayr Mount is one of the state's most stunning plantation homes from the Federal era (c.1815). Painstakingly restored and furnished with period antiques, it offers guided tours and a one-mile Poet's Walk around the estate.

Morehead-Patterson Bell Tower *(opposite)*

The bell tower at UNC, a gift of two university alumni in 1931, rises 172 feet above campus grounds. Every hour, the familiar sound of the carillon's bells is a melodic reminder of the great history of America's first state university.

Unsung Founders Memorial *(top and bottom)*

The base of this memorial is held up by three-hundred figures depicting African-Americans who were instrumental in the building of UNC. Five stone seats circle the table.

The Old Well *(opposite)*

A long-standing superstition of the country's oldest university states that if a student drinks from the fountain at the school's old well on the first day of classes, he or she is destined for straight A's.

The text on the plaque reads:

MARGARET LANE
CEMETERY

Before 1852 to 1931

Well before the Civil War this sacred site was set aside as a burial
place for local slaves and their families. It remained active until
the early nineteen thirties.

Dedicated 1987

Margaret Lane Cemetery *(above)*

The Margaret Lane Cemetery in
Chapel Hill is an historic burial ground.
This cemetery, with its rough and broken fieldstone markers, contains the
only known records of many slaves
who lived and died in the county.

U.N.C. Cemetery *(opposite)*

This pastoral cemetery tells stories of
the university and the town that grew
up around it. Students often find it a
good place for quiet contemplation.
The oldest grave dates back to 1798,
and all the remaining plots are taken.

Playmakers Repertory Company

A professional theater company of
U.N.C.'s Department of Dramatic Arts,
the Playmakers Repertory Company
gives university drama students a
unique opportunity to mentor in all
aspects of professional playmaking.

Historic Playmakers Theater

Built in 1851 in the style of a Greek Revival temple, this distinctive UNC structure was the performance space of the original Carolina Playmakers who were instrumental in bringing the folk drama genre to American theatre.

Varsity Theater, Chapel Hill *(above)*

With its familiar neon marquis, the oldest remaining movie theater is part of the charm of East Franklin Street, the heart of this college town. Restaurants and music shops add to the area's popularity with students.

Paul Green Theater *(opposite)*

This university theater is named after renowned graduate and Pulitzer Prize-winning playwright, Paul Green, whose realistic plays portrayed the lives of African-Americans and white tenant farmers in the South.

PAUL GREEN

THEATRE

PAUL GREEN
1894 - 1981
Dramatist - Teacher - Humanist

Carolina Class of 1921
Pulitzer Prize for Drama 1927
Broadway's Theatre Hall of Fame 1993

Bust by William E. Hipp
Provided by the Lillian Hughes Prince Fund

Morehead Planetarium and
Science Center

A gift of UNC alumnus John Morehead
III, the university planetarium is one of
the nation's largest, with a 68-foot,
domed Star Theater and state-of-the-
art star projector.

Mysteries of the Universe *(top)*

Over 100,000 people attend sky shows at the Star Theater, where the mysteries of the universe unfold before their eyes. Planetarium staff thrills the audience with tales of lunar landings, black holes and the Big Bang.

Planetarium Rotunda *(bottom)*

Fine art adorns the walls of the planetarium's striking rotunda. Center-stage is a statue of distinguished UNC alumnus, James K. Polk, who went on to become the eleventh president of the United States.

Memorial Hall

After an $18-million transformation of
the 1931 structure, the UNC Memorial
Hall re-opened in 2005 as a state-of-
the-art venue for world-class music,
dance and theater. The North Carolina
Symphony performs here regularly.

Memorial Hall, UNC

The 1,625-seat concert hall is part of UNC's new Arts Commons, which extends from the university's front door down to the Historic Playmakers Theatre, a symbolic intersection of the arts on campus and in the community.

A Home of Great Thinkers

The historic Horace Williams House has been home to outspoken university professors, including Benjamin Hedrick, who was fired by UNC-Chapel Hill due to his outspoken opposition to slavery in the 1850's.

Horace Williams House

This historic Chapel Hill house evolved over several architectural periods. The central farmhouse section of the house (c.1840) has original pine floor boards, mantel, and window surrounds.

Entertaining in Style (above)

The parlor and entrance hall of the
Horace-Williams House were built in
the 1880's, and are decorated with
popular furnishings and details of
the period. The dark, parquet ceiling
displays meticulous craftsmanship.

Horace Williams Portrait (opposite)

Horace Williams was a beloved philo-
sophy professor at UNC-Chapel Hill
for fifty years. Many nights, he would
meet with his students in the front
parlor to engage in lively philosophic
discussions. One student, novelist
Thomas Wolfe, called him a "great
teacher" in his classic *You Can't Go
Home Again.* Fully restored, the
house is a cultural treasure and an
exhibition space for North Carolina
artists.

Chapel Hill Museum *(top)*

After a noble fire-fighting career, this 1914 Model T fire truck was officially retired. It was the first motorized fire truck, complete with hoses, which shortened the time to get to fires and increased the water's power and reach.

Character and Characters *(bottom)*

Opened in 1997, the museum presents an average of twelve exhibits of different scope and size to represent "the character and characters of Chapel Hill." Education programs reach 2,000 local students annually.

Chapel Hill Museum Exhibits

Attracting 20,000 visitors annually, exhibits in this young museum focus on all aspects of Chapel Hill life and history—from "Lost and Found," a community art project, to a collection of historic pottery pieces.

North Carolina Botanical Gardens *(above)*   **Quiet Haven** *(opposite)*

Encompassing nearly one-thousand acres, including a nature preserve, the botanical gardens are a leading force in native plant education and conservation in the southeastern United States.

Shake off a stressful day at the office or study without interruption on a secluded bench under the shade of the botanical gardens' towering trees. The beauty and serenity provide a natural quiet haven.

Garden Visitors *(above)*

In the middle of the gardens, a quaint birdhouse attracts two feathery visitors while a curious boy can't resist putting his hands in the dirt. The gardens blend formal display areas with natural areas and hiking trails.

Piedmont Nature Trail *(opposite)*

The Piedmont Nature Trail is where hikers can treck a two-mile trail through eighty-eight acres of forest typical of central North Carolina. Benches provide a place to stop and enjoy nature's abundant beauty.

Coker Aboretum *(above)*

Now part of the North Carolina Botanical Gardens, the arboretum dates back to 1903, when William Coker, UNC's first botany professor, turned a boggy pasture into an outdoor classroom featuring native plantings.

Charlie "Choo Choo" Justice *(opposite)*

Next to the football stadium where Charlie Justice made history in the late 1940's, the statue of this all-American tailback rises in his honor. Justice was one of the most celebrated college players of his time.

Carrboro Farmers Market

This nationally-recognized market delights its customers with free tastings of melons, strawberries, and tomatoes. "Chef's Choice" is a special event where local chefs serve dishes created with fresh market produce.

Locally Grown *(top)*

Located just a few miles from downtown Chapel Hill, everything available in this nationally-acclaimed market is grown or produced within a 50-mile radius and sold by the same people who grew it.

Cream of the Crop *(bottom)*

The market has sold fresh fruits, vegetables, prepared foods, flowers and crafts since 1974. Recently, Audubon Magazine voted Carrboro one of the country's "Top-Ten Cream of the Crop" farmers markets in the nation.

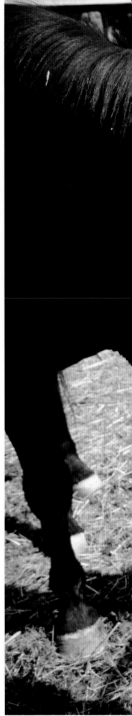

Spence's Farm

This historic family farm has a new life
as a unique teaching environment.
The curriculum is built around life on
a working farm so that children can
learn the joy of nature and working
with farm animals.

In Touch

Spence's Farm is an ideal, back-to-basics setting for children to experience enjoyable barn-yard activities such as horse-back riding or making pottery.

Patterson's Mill Country Store

A detour off the main road in Chapel
Hill leads to a special treat at the end
of this rutted, country lane. This is an
authentic, turn-of-the-century country
store, doctor's office and pharmacy,
filled with memorabilia and souvenirs.

Old Time Medicine

An off-the-beaten-track treasure, the country store features artifacts from the Patterson's Mill community, including the vials, potions, and medical tools used by pharmacists and doctors at the turn of the 20th century.

Chapel Hill's Main Drag

Nicknamed "the Southern Part of Heaven," Chapel Hill is a great place for a leisurely walk, whether exploring UNC's beautifully landscaped campus or strolling down Franklin Street, the city's main drag.

College Town Center

Beginning at the planetarium and
running parallel to UNC's campus,
Franklin Street bustles with the sights
and sounds of students who come
here for its quaint shops, music stores,
cheap eateries, and Varsity theatre.

Stories on the Wall *(above)*

History marches along the side of a
brick building in this artistic interpre-
tation of Chapel Hill's rich heritage.
An eclectic mix of outdoor mural
styles dot the Raleigh-Durham-Chapel
Hill area.

Hillsborough Courthouse Clock *(opposite)*

Historic Hillsborough was once the
state capital of North Carolina. Built in
the 1840's, this courthouse features an
18th-century clock that continues to
keep perfect time.

124

Apple Chill Festival *(top, bottom, opposite)*

The "Kids Zone" at the Apple Chill street festival is a source of pure delight. There is plenty for adults, too, from paintings, pottery, jewelry and woodworking to live music performances and international food courts.

A springtime arts and crafts street fair, Apple Chill provides a great outdoor venue for area talent. Each year the Chapel Hill fair becomes increasingly popular, attracting record-breaking crowds of 30,000-plus.